HONOLULU HI
AUG
24
2002
96820

FIRST DAY OF ISSUE
DUKE PAOA KAHANAMOKU

Duke
PAOA KAHANAMOKU
HO'OLAULE'A

Duke
A Great Hawaiian

Sandra Kimberley Hall

3565 Harding Avenue
Honolulu, Hawai'i 96816
toll free: (800) 910-2377
phone: (808) 734-7159
fax: (808) 732-3627
BessPress.com

Design: Carol Colbath
Cover photograph: International Swimming Hall of Fame
Aloha print: Duke Kahanamoku Made in Hawaii by Kahala EE

Library of Congress Cataloging-in-Publication Data

Hall, Sandra Kimberley.
  Duke : a great Hawaiian / Sandra
Kimberley Hall ; foreword by
Wilmer C. Morris.
     p. cm.
  Includes illustrations, bibliography.
  ISBN 978-1-57306-230-5
  1. Kahanamoku, Duke, 1890-1968.
2. Swimmers - Hawaii - Biography.
3. Surfers - Hawaii - Biography.
4. Hawaiians - Biography. I. Title.
GV838.K35.H35 2004   796.9-dc21

© 2004 by Bess Press, Inc.

Fifth printing in 2012

Printed in China

The author is grateful to Malama Pono Ltd. for permission to use
images of Duke Paoa Kahanamoku.

To the children of Hawai'i-*nei,*

because you are all Duke's children

Foreword

Duke Paoa Kahanamoku taught me to swim when I was five years old at my grandfather's house at Puʻuloa, the entrance to Pearl Harbor.

I have had the privilege to know the Kahanamoku family all my life. This long acquaintance gave me a special entrée to "Paoa," as he asked me to call him.

Physically impressive, he was a magnificent Polynesian—handsome, magnetic, with an aura that drew all eyes when he entered a room. He was also a natural leader and the ultimate authority when conflicts arose on Waikīkī Beach. His 20 years of Olympic competition did more to put Hawaiʻi "on the map" than anyone before or since.

This world celebrity remained true to his old-fashioned upbringing and the values learned in his youth. He was always honest and humble, modestly aware of his impact on people. At his core he was Hawaiian. His most trusted friends were those he grew up with. He reflected a quiet dignity and was a good judge of character. He was patient with people who wanted to shake his hand, be in his presence. He was never *mahaʻoi*—it was not Hawaiian to be inhospitable and discourteous. He had an inner strength that was warming and calming to those around him. He was comfortable with himself.

Some of my most cherished memories are of leaning against a canoe, warmed by the afternoon sun, listening to Paoa reminisce about growing up in Kālia, simple stories told with great emotion.

Visiting him at home at the end of his life, I'd sit next to him on the sofa, looking out at Maunalua Bay and Koko Head. He'd take my hand, recalling memories. Sometimes we just sat there, and no words were spoken.

How fortunate I was to know him as I did!

Aloha, Paoa.

WILMER C. MORRIS

Duke in his thirties. This photo was used on the cover of the millennial issue of *Surfer* Magazine when Duke was voted Surfer of the Century.

*H*awai'i-*nei*'s most famous native son, after King Kamehameha the Great, is the full-blooded Duke Paoa Kahanamoku (1890–1968).

He is the greatest aquatic sportsman the world has ever known.

This stamp commemorating the twenty-fifth anniversary of Hawai'i statehood depicts a typical Polynesian voyaging canoe.

*D*uke was a direct descendant through his maternal lineage, the Paoas, of the legendary Vikings of the Sunrise who settled the Hawaiian Islands. Still a famous name in the Marquesas, Rapa Nui, Tahiti, and New Zealand, the Paoas are arguably the most remarkable navigators the world has seen.

It was Duke's destiny to be an outstanding waterman.

Honolulu, circa 1900.

*I*n old Hawai'i, times of relative tranquility alternated with times of bloodshed between warring tribes. When Kamehameha the Great united the Islands in 1810, a short-lived peace prevailed. Ten years later, New England missionaries arrived. They frowned on the "savage" culture, and almost succeeded in obliterating it. Surfing, dancing, celebrating, and music all but vanished. Even clothing and house design changed.

The death knell for the native-born sounded with the arrival of *haole* ("strangers"), many of them merchants and traders, who brought diseases like measles, whooping cough, smallpox, and diphtheria to which the *kanaka maoli* had no defenses. The full-blooded population was decimated, plummeting from perhaps 800,000 to 1 million in 1778 to 82,000 in 1850.

A missionary preaching to Native Hawaiians.

*T*o a Hawaiian, the essence of life is *hā,* the breath. Many important words are based on *hā*: *mahalo, hānai, 'ohana,* and *Hawai'i.* The most important is *aloha.* Its practice was so innate to being, self-definition, laws, and culture, it helped Hawaiians survive the overwhelming chaos.

•••

aloha

1. Love, affection, compassion, mercy, sympathy, pity, kindness, sentiment, grace, charity; 2. Greeting, salutation, regards; 3. Sweetheart, lover, loved one; 4. Beloved, loving, kind, compassionate, charitable, lovable; 5. To love, be fond of; 6. To show kindness, mercy, pity, charity, affection; 7. To venerate; to remember with affection; 8. To greet, hail.

Queen Victoria's second son, the Duke of Edinburgh.

*F*or half a century there had been little collective cause for celebration, until July 21, 1869, when Prince Alfred, the Duke of Edinburgh, arrived on the *Galatea* on a goodwill visit. His mother, Queen Victoria of Great Britain, was like family to Hawaiian royalty.

The same day, a baby boy was born to Kahanamoku senior and Kapiolani Kaoeha at Chief Paki's residence. Paki's wife Konia was a descendant of Kamehameha's, and the Kahanamoku family had served as *kahu,* trusted advisers, for generations of the Kamehamehas.

Before Alfred came ashore, the *Galatea*'s cannon saluted the Hawaiian flag. A welcoming volley replied. Paki's daughter, Princess Bernice Pauahi, who was cradling the baby, chose the name "Duke," in honor of the Duke of Edinburgh.

Twenty-one years later, Duke Halapu and his wife Julia would name their first surviving child Duke Paoa Kahanamoku.

Duke diving from the 100-foot-high spar of a sailing vessel in Honolulu Harbor.

*H*e Oli Komo Aloha

A Welcome Chant

Pā mai ka leo aloha o Hawaiʻi nei,
    Hawaiʻi's voice of aloha calls forth,

I hoʻokipa i ke ahi o nā ʻalapa o ʻAmelika hui pū ʻia,
    To welcome the flame of America's Triathlon athletes,

Eia pū hoʻi, ʻeā
    And behold too

Hoʻomaikaʻi mai ka wailua o Pāoa Kahanamoku
    The spirit of Duke Paoa Kahanamoku inspires

I hoʻopaipai a i lanakila ai, ʻeā!
    In support of victory!

Composed and translated by Kalani Meinecke, April 10, 2004

Downtown Honolulu about the time of Duke Paoa Kahanamoku's birth in 1890.

*D*uke Halapu's wife, Julia Paakonia Paoa, gave birth to Duke Paoa on August 24, 1890, in a time of economic turbulence and intense political maneuvering by *haole*.

When Princess Pauahi died without heirs, the Kamehameha ruling lineage died also. The worldwide economic depression hit Hawai'i hard, causing high unemployment. Because women's fashion no longer dictated wearing waist-defining corsets with whalebone stays, and because whale oil was being replaced with more easily acquired fuel sources, whaling, which employed one in five Hawaiians, was dying out. Hawai'i's sugar plantations were in their infancy.

No longer entitled to live on a royal estate, Duke Halapu found employment as a delivery clerk and hack driver.

A typical scene in the 1890s in Honolulu—sailing ships giving way to steam, and a visiting militia drill.

*I*n 1891, when Duke was five months old, King David Kalākaua died. Hawaiians agonized over whether the monarchy could survive, while *haole* clamored for change.

Honolulu was tense—whisperings and fleeting shadows in the streets at night, and uniformed, armed militia marching in the day.

In 1893, the young Kahanamoku family moved to Kālia, Waikīkī, to live near Julia's parents and her Paoa *'ohana*.

Ducks on the mud flats of Kālia.

At one time more than one hundred Paoas were living in Kālia. Duke counted thirty-one Paoa cousins—instant playmates!—of his own generation. None of the homes were fancy, like the merchants' homes in downtown Honolulu, but the sea and the land produced a cornucopia of crabs, *'opihi*, fish, squid, *limu*, octopuses, taro, coconuts, bananas, and sweet potatoes.

Over time, the ancient fishponds became rice fields and duck ponds, which drained into the stream that cut across the Paoa land and emptied into mud-flats that stank at low tide.

Today, the Hilton Hawaiian Village occupies much of this land; Paoa *iwi* rest beneath the *'āina* that sustained them.

Queen Lydia Liliʻuokalani, Hawaiʻi's last reigning monarch.

*P*olitical unrest escalated.

It was hard to determine from one week to the next what was happening—a maelstrom swirled within and without:

• In faraway Washington, D.C., a U.S. president contradicted his predecessor as to Hawai'i's sovereignty status.

• In Honolulu, Queen Lili'uokalani tried to promulgate a new constitution but was rebuffed and dethroned. A counterrevolution failed; the queen was imprisoned and despite anguished appeals to the U.S. Congress, she was deposed in 1893. The nights were heavy with brokenhearted wailing.

No longer an independent nation, Hawai'i became a provisional republic.

Duke was probably oblivious to the turmoil—or maybe it prepared and steeled him for what would later come. By the time of Duke's death in 1968, he had lived through monarchy, provisional republic, republic, territory, martial law, and statehood.

Idyllic Waikīkī in the late 1890s, near Kapiʻolani Park.

*D*uke was a typical *keiki*—frolicking in the sand, climbing trees, playing with his cousins.

He learned to swim, naked, not much more than a toddler, the old way: " 'My father and uncle just threw me into the water from an outrigger canoe. I had to swim or else.' "

And he learned to surf, by trial and error: " 'We keikis taught each other.' "

Before the missionaries, surfing, perfected over hundreds of years, was an integral part of Hawaiian life. To be a wave warrior was to be a hero. Surfing stories were woven into myths and legends. Boards were expertly crafted, highly prized, cared for, and handed down through generations. Although surfing was not totally extinguished, it had all but disappeared in a generation. In 1898, an observer saw just one surfer at Waikīkī.

At the turn of the twentieth century, a handful of individuals experimented again with surfing, asking the *kūpuna* to share their knowledge.

Duke's mother, Julia Kahanamoku. She is probably in her late fifties in this undated photograph. She died in 1936.

When he was seven or eight years old and could competently swim and surf, Duke spent every possible moment in the ocean, his playground. There were shells to dive for, octopuses to spear, rock pools to explore, and underwater breath-holding contests. He also learned to body surf and to dive. The older children supervised the little ones.

There was always something special to see: floating on his back, the misty rain curtains and rainbows over the Koʻolau Mountains; or lying on his board, the tall-masted ships with billowing sails gliding in from the farthest corners of the globe on the horizon.

Duke in his late teens.

Ku no i ke keʻa.
Like father, like son.

Much was expected of a person who bore the name Paoa or the name Kahanamoku. And even more was expected of a person who carried both of these names and was the first surviving *hiapo* (grandchild) of the two mighty lineages.

Duke's father was rapidly promoted from desk clerk through the ranks to captain of the Second Watch.

*A*t six years of age, Duke began kindergarten. Teachers caned students to remind them to speak only English. The mellifluous Hawaiian language was *kapu*, banned.

After elementary school, he attended the Kamehameha Industrial School for Boys, but quit before graduating. In a Lowell Thomas radio interview on July 27, 1949, he said that he spent his time after school "trying to earn money—selling newspapers, shining shoes, carrying ice, and doing just about anything that would bring in some pocket money."

His father now worked at the Honolulu Police Department.

Duke briefly returned to McKinley High, but once again did not graduate. His diver's paycheck was needed to help pay the family's bills, now that he had three sisters and five brothers.

Hui Nalu. *Back row, third from right,* Duke; *front row, second from left,* Dude Miller.

*S*erene Waikīkī changed forever when the Moana Hotel opened in 1901, and explosive changes continued through the decade:

- The Hawaii Promotion Committee (HPC), the precursor to the Hawaii Visitors Bureau, was formed in 1903.

- A steady stream of journalists arrived, including best-selling author Jack London, who wrote about the "new" sport of surfing.

- Political and economic stability, and an influx of new population, led to merchants' building homes along Waikīkī, restricting public access to the beach.

- In 1907 George Freeth, Duke's mentor, left for California, where he taught the locals to "walk on water." He promoted both surfing and Hawai'i and paved the way for Duke's visits to California.

- The Outrigger Canoe and Surf Club was formed by *haole* in 1908 to ensure both beach access and that "the native sports do not die out."

- The same year, in defiance at being excluded from the *haole* Outrigger, and to have their expertise recognized, a group of young, mainly *kanaka maoli,* but also *hapa-haole* and *haole* formed the Hui Nalu, Club of the Waves. Duke was member number 2.

- Tourism grew steadily. HPC reported that 1909 was its best year ever with its average of 300 visitors per month.

Duke at 21.

*I*n 1910 an event of interest exclusively to Hawai'i would change Duke's life and Hawai'i and would reverberate worldwide. After lengthy debate, Honolulu's many sports clubs voted to create the Amateur Athletic Union-Hawai'i. Its creation made Hawai'i's athletes eligible for AAU national participation and, maybe one day, participation in the Olympics.

The first AAU-Hawai'i sanctioned contest, a swim meet, was held the next year on August 12, 1911. Duke's performance—clipping 4.6 seconds off the world freestyle record of one minute flat for the 100-yard open water, was so startling that mainland AAU officials were skeptical.

They questioned whether the floats (to mark the end of the race in the harbor) might have drifted together several hours after measuring; the tide, although reported as not favorable, might have actually helped him; all four judges' stopwatches really recorded the same time; Duke was a complete unknown.

Decision: Disallowed.

Duke Kahanamoku and His Record Breaking Pedals

Some feet—no? They belong to Duke Kahanamoku, champion swimmer of the world. Of course they are really not this large; it is the distortion of perspective by the camera that makes them appear so. And they say that the camera does not lie! The picture was taken in Los Angeles when Duke recently took part in a swimming meet. Kahanamoku is very proud of his feet; they have propelled him to many a victory.

Pacific Commercial Advertiser, September 26, 1914.

With individual donations ranging from 25 cents, $1,500 was raised to send Duke and three others to the AAU National Swimming Championship. Accompanying Duke were distance swimmer Vincent "Zen" Genovese, manager Lew Henderson, originally from Philadelphia, who had valuable East Coast contacts, and Duke's best friend, the Hui Nalu commodore, Edward K. "Dude" Miller.

They left in early February 1912. Nobody could have predicted that Duke would be gone for nine months, and that he would return as the world champ.

Initially, his East Coast races were a disaster. According to a *Los Angeles Times* article, "He did a foolhardy feat. He did not give himself time to get acclimatized. He climbed out of a train, travel worn, and plunged right into the tank." In his first race, he led by five laps, but suffered a cramp.

Within days he had learned how to make a fast start, how to turn at the end of the pool, and how to breathe through his mouth. It took hard work for him to secure a place on the Olympic team.

A familiar sight poolside was Duke playing a guitar or ukulele. This photo was taken in 1918 in Chicago.

*D*uke strummed his ukulele poolside at the Stockholm Olympics to stay calm. The competition at his first Olympics would be fierce in the 100-meter freestyle, especially from the Aussie champ Cecil Healy.

Duke won his heat, but there was a snafu when Duke and others did not show up for their semifinal race. Healy could have snared the gold, but he petitioned the judges to reschedule Duke's semifinal race. When they declined, Healy refused to swim. The judges faced a unique dilemma, and relented. Duke swam in a special semifinal and then beat Healy in world-record time, by just a whisker.

Duke also won a silver medal for the 4 x 200-meter freestyle relay.

Duke and Hawai'i were headlined on newspaper front pages the world over. He was the center of attention as much for his quiet demeanor and lack of pretension as for his phenomenal crawl stroke.

A modest Duke receives his Olympic laurel wreath from King Gustav V.

*O*n his mainland return, Duke made good on a promise to teach his East Coast friends how to surf. They had shown him true aloha, taking no money for the training, food, and three-months' lodging that had made his Stockholm win possible.

After what seemed an interminable train and boat trip, finally! Diamond Head.

When the *Wilhelmina* was sighted, Fort Ruger's cannon blast was the signal thousands were waiting for. People scurried from shops, offices, schools, and homes to the wharf. Trains, tugs, and factories blew their whistles.

The *Honolulu Star-Bulletin* reported that Duke had "lost none of the modesty that won him hosts of friends everywhere he went. It only dawned on many of his fellow passengers who he was when the boat steamed into the harbor."

Duke nattily dressed on a fishing trip in California. Fishing was a lifelong hobby.

*D*uke was hired as a rodman (surveyor) for the Honolulu Water Department. After work, he was a familiar sight, training at Waikīkī.

Honoluluans finally got to see how he measured up against mainland champs in June 1913. Not one, but *three* surveyors measured the harbor course to avoid a repetition of 1911.

Duke did not disappoint the fans. He set a new world record for the open-water 100-yard freestyle, broke Hawaiian and national records for the 50-yard and 440-yard, and won the 220-yard race. Spectators threw their hats into the air, waved handkerchiefs, and yelled till they were hoarse.

Duke in New Zealand.

*T*hen he was off to California in July for the Pacific Coast Swimming Championships. Newspaper headlines proclaimed, "The Duke Visits." He thrilled the crowd of 6,000 in his first race, demolishing the 75-yard-freestyle world record, broke his own world record for the 100-yard freestyle, won the 440-yard freestyle, the 220-yard freestyle, the 50-yard freestyle, and the 50-yard backstroke.

He had launched a revolution. Everyone wanted to learn the Kahanamoku Kick.

Duke and Freeth traveled to Los Angeles and wowed the crowds with their surfing. Duke decided if he were offered a job, he would relocate to California.

George Cunha, manager Francis Evans, and Duke during their trip to
Australia and New Zealand, 1914–1915.

*N*ineteen fourteen dawned uneasily with the planet teetering on the brink of war. Even Hawai'i was affected, when German ships were seized in Honolulu Harbor.

For the last time before the Great War, mainland champs came to swim in the annual Mid-Pacific Carnival. In June, and again in October, Duke headed a Hawaiian contingent that competed at San Francisco's Sutro Baths.

Duke, Hui Nalu, and Hawai'i once again proved they were the world's best swimmers.

Duke visited Australia to keep his 1912 Olympiad promise. A world-class sprinter, George Cunha, accompanied him. They were well-matched, making the races very exciting for the spectators. More records were broken in 1914–15 than in any other season in the Australian Swimming Association's 24-year history.

Although Duke participated in more than 50 races, he is best remembered for his surfing at Freshwater, a Sydney beach, Christmas 1914.

Duke and admirers at Freshwater Surf Life Saving Club, Christmas 1914.

$\mathcal{A}$ustralians certainly knew about surfing before Duke's 1914–15 visit. Before air travel, passengers en route to the United States stopped in Honolulu for a week or more. But the different shore-breaks at home made Aussies' attempts to "surf-shoot" futile.

When Duke taught Aussies how to shape a board and then to choose and to ride a wave, they became instant converts.

•••

At "Freshie Beach," people still talk about Duke's visit as though it were recent, not nine decades ago. His statue overlooks a commemorative park and a walk of fame, and his original board is a surfer's shrine. It is probably the world's most loved board.

Australia has a special place in its heart for Duke. His visit came just 13 years after its states had federated into an uneasy alliance. He helped the nation forge its identity, largely based on sports and its relationship to the sur-rounding ocean.

•••

Then he visited New Zealand, broke his own world record in the 50-yard freestyle, and reintroduced surfing. A high point was meeting his Polynesian kin, the Maori.

Duke took his training seriously. Here he looks 28, but is 38 years old.

The 1916 Berlin Games, for which Duke and others had trained for four years, were cancelled. To soothe Hawai'i's crushing disappointment, Honolulu was invited to host the 1917 AAU National Championship in the fall. Eight Illinois champions visited. An anonymous letter writer warned in the *Los Angeles Times,* "the great Hawaiian [Duke] has probably seen his best day."

The writer was wrong.

First, Duke broke his own world record in the 100-yard freestyle. A bigger surprise came in the 220-yard race, in which Duke had been last to start. By 120 yards, the record holder, Norman Ross, had the lead. By 200, Duke surged ahead to win!

At meet's end, the tally showed three world records.

Fifty years later Duke wrote that it was "the greatest aquatic event in Hawai'i's history."

In 1917 he also rode his massive longboard 1 1/8th miles at Waikīkī, an unparalleled feat in modern surfing.

A not uncommon sight was men and women knitting scarves and sweaters for U.S. servicemen in Europe. Duke was described as an expert knitter.

*D*uring 1918, hundreds of thousands of people in 30 mainland cities turned out to see Duke and two other Hawaiians swim against their local "boys" to raise money for U.S. War Bonds.

Antwerp, Belgium, was awarded the Games for 1920, but was ill prepared following almost ceaseless bombardment for four brutal years. The aquatic venue was a filthy canal with wooden edges, the best Antwerp could do.

Duke won two gold medals—for the 100-meter freestyle and 4 x 200-meter relay. He also played on the U.S. water polo team, which placed fourth. The water was so cold he turned purple, he said.

Duke was swimming even better at age 30. Hawai'i's 7 swimmers entered 26 contests before, during, and after the Olympics, and won 59 medals. The HPC was exuberant. Members kept their fingers crossed that shipping would soon return to normal to take advantage of the free publicity for Hawai'i.

Duke in an unidentified movie role with an unidentified actress. Apparently he is teaching her how to swim, although she is wearing shoes.

*I*n 1922, Duke's dream of living in California came true when he secured a movie contract with Paramount Pictures. His manager worked hard to get suitable roles for Duke, but he was faced with two problems. Duke could not receive money for swimming—which is what the public wanted to see—because of AAU rules. The second problem in Haolewood, as Duke called Hollywood, was casting. Directors had narrow and stereotypical ideas about appropriate roles for a dark-skinned man. He appeared in about 30 movies, bridging the silent movies and the "talkies." By nature, he was more suited to the silent movies.

To pay the bills between movie roles, Duke worked as a lifeguard and as a mechanic. Weekends he spent surfing.

Today, as a world champion, he would probably receive millions of dollars in endorsements.

And, far away in Boston, a teenage girl saw Duke's photo in a movie magazine and fell in love with him; this story must wait its turn.

Duke and Viola Hartmann (later Cady), tandem surfing at Laguna Beach, California, in 1922.

$\mathcal{L}$ife was not always easy for a dark-skinned man on the mainland. Champion diver and swimmer Viola Hartmann knew Duke when he lived in Los Angeles and was one of the most recognized people in the world. She said,

> He was always quiet and lovely and agreeable. He was very easy going. He never tried to stand out. I remember going to a swim meet at Lake Arrowhead, and stopping at a restaurant. The waitress said, "We don't serve Negroes. You need to go out," gesturing towards the door. Duke started to ever so slightly get up gracefully, but we all spoke in unison, "He's not a Negro. He's a Hawaiian and that is not the same." The waitress was very puzzled, but served us, and him. So Duke stayed. I'm sure he would have avoided a fuss and gone and sat in the car, because that is what he was like.

Duke was quietly integrating sports 30 years before the major-league baseball teams allowed African-American Jackie Robinson to play.

Duke welcomes Johnny Weissmuller to Honolulu. In this photo, Johnny is 17 and Duke is 31.

*B*y 1923, Duke had been beaten only once in four years.

But competition was nibbling at his heels in the form of Johnny Weissmuller, 13 years younger, and his own brother Sam, 12 years younger. In pre-Olympic meets it was anyone's guess who would go on to win the gold.

Weissmuller won at the U.S. Nationals, and again at the 1924 Paris Olympics with a world record of 59 seconds in the 100 meters. Duke took second and Sam third. Duke accepted his defeat graciously and was proud that America had won all first three places.

Duke historian Earl Maikahikinapāmaikalā Tenn says,

> Most Olympic swimmers compete in their first Olympics as teenagers and retire well before they are 30. Duke was an exception. He was unusually old to be an Olympian. He competed in his first Olympics and won his first gold medals at age 22. He competed in Olympics until he was 42, with qualifying times as good as or better than those of his younger days. His span of 21 years of Olympic participation is not likely to be beaten in aquatic sports or perhaps any sports.

Johnny Weissmuller became the winningest record holder in American history, with 36 national titles.

The New York Times crowed after the Games, "A generation ago swimming was not a special American accomplishment." They quoted a French official who said "[The Paris Olympics, 1924] now looked like an American holiday." The United States won 13 of 17 swimming events, a total of 217 points, far ahead of the next three countries combined. "The United States must appear as a superman nation to the crowd at [the Games]."

The credit of course belonged mainly to Duke, who had electrified interest in swimming in 1912. The new world champ, Johnny Weissmuller, acknowledged this: "I learned it all from him." He and Duke, the champ whose throne he usurped, became lifelong friends, which rarely happens in any sport.

Duke wearing the *Thelma* heroism medal. Paramount Pictures released this photo-graph to publicize his 1925 movies *Adventure*, *Lord Jim*, and *Pony Express*.

*O*ne weekend in June 1925, Duke was at Corona del Mar with several surfing friends. They watched the *Thelma*, a 40-foot, 5-ton for-hire pleasure yacht, leave the Newport breakwater. Suddenly, mountainous waves swept seventeen fishing buddies overboard.

Duke and his friends paddled out to the flailing men. Duke made three trips to and from the beach, rescuing eight men. Owen Hale and Gerard Vultee rescued another four. Five bodies were retrieved. The Newport police chief said, " 'The Duke's performance was the most superhuman rescue act. . . . Many more would have drowned, but for the quick action of the Hawaiian swimmer.' "

In his autobiography Duke wrote, "Good sometimes comes from the worst of tragedies. . . . Boards became standard equipment on the emergency rescue trucks as well as at the towers."

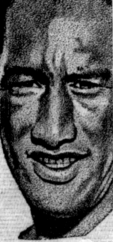

Duke Kahanamoku

. . . member of the crew of yacht Manuiwa . . . will be glad to greet all his old friends at either of his two service stations — on Nuuanu St. or on Kalakaua Ave.

DUKE P. KAHANAMOKU

UNION OIL PRODUCTS

TWO STATIONS . . .

Nuuanu Street at Pauoa Road

Kalakaua Avenue, opposite the Royal Hawaiian Hotel

Aloha! President Roosevelt

Honolulu Star-Bulletin, July 26, 1934.

*D*uke had his sights set on the 1928 Amsterdam Olympics. His speed was improving, and maybe he could catch Weissmuller. His dreams were dashed when he got sick and he did not make the U.S. team. Then the movie studio cut back because of the Great Depression. He was uncertain what to do.

He visited Honolulu, with much fanfare, to christen the Waikiki War Memorial Natatorium on his 37th birthday in 1927. William Rawlins, one of AAU-Hawai'i's pioneers, said, " 'Opening the Natatorium without Duke would have been like having a luau without poi, leaving out the main ingredient.' "

The Hawai'i State Legislature appealed to him to return home, but he discovered that the promised position, as superintendent of the new City Hall, was a janitor's job. He was the butt of jokes. Then he was "unceremoniously kicked out" by the newly elected Democratic majority on the Board of Supervisors.

Friends helped him lease two service stations. Once again he was ridiculed, when the former world champ pumped gas and cleaned windshields. He seemed to take it in stride. Fortunately he had his *'ohana*, his friends, and a new interest—surfboard design.

Tom Blake became a champion swimmer, surfer, and inventor because of Duke.
Here they pose with the first longboard with a fin.

*D*uke's aloha boomeranged. A person Duke had met by chance in 1920 would now have a big impact on his life.

From dairyland Wisconsin, 18-year-old Tom Blake was living in Detroit when he saw a newsreel about the then much discussed American victories in Antwerp.

To his surprise, standing in the theater lobby was the world champion himself, with his fellow Olympians, who had stopped in to see themselves on newsreel.

Blake wrote, "Duke shook my hand. He held out his big, soft paw, and gave me a firm, hearty handshake. I took it as my own personal invitation to Hawai'i."

Blake moved to Los Angeles, took up swimming, surfing, and lifeguarding, and renewed his chance acquaintanceship with Duke.

Then he moved to Hawai'i, becoming one of surfing's most accomplished innovators, experimenting with fins, different woods, and even sails.

Blake and Duke enjoyed experimenting with ancient designs and modern compounds. They worked on hollow boards and reintroduced the *olo* (longboard), from models in the Bishop Museum.

The last photograph of a graceful Duke surfing, on his 64th birthday, August 24, 1954. It is autographed by Duke to his manager Kimo Wilder McVay.

*T*om Blake wrote, "To see Duke coming in at Waikiki on his long *olo* board was to see surfriding at its best. . . . To me, the Duke is . . . the man by which to measure the race, the surfrider by which to measure the surfriders of all time."

Now he was home, Duke rarely missed a day without going swimming, surfing, or bodysurfing. The ocean kept him centered. It washed away any hurts and cleansed his spirit.

In a *San Francisco Chronicle* interview, Duke gave this advice to youngsters afraid of the sea: "Relax. Let your muscles be soft. When they tighten up from fear, you are as heavy as a rock and you sink. Controlled breathing, more than anything else, is the secret. If you have only a third of a lungful of air, it will keep you up."

Duke's niece, Jo-Anne Kahanamoku, said that Duke liked nothing better than to be with his *'ohana*, and to eat traditional foods. No matter which famous celebrity he had just dined with, at what fancy restaurant, poi, *lomi-lomi,* corned beef, chopped onion, and a strawberry orange soda tasted best to him.

Duke bodysurfing at Makapu'u Beach. Note his enormous shoulders and arm span.

$\mathcal{A}$t age 42, Duke played as an alternate on the U.S. water polo team at the Los Angeles Olympics, winning a bronze medal. This brought his tally to six Olympic medals, *and* he still held a world record—after 21 years—for the 50-yard freestyle!

What did the future hold in store? Although his Olympic and Hollywood careers were behind him, he was continuing his role as Hawai'i's unofficial, unpaid Ambassador of Aloha.

In 1934 he crewed on Harold G. Dillingham's yacht, which won the grueling Trans Pacific race. It was probably during this trip that a "bug was put into his ear" about running for public office. Dillingham and his friends knew they had a shoo-in candidate.

Later that year, Duke ran for the City and County of Honolulu Sheriff's Office and won, a scenario that would be repeated every two years for 26 years.

Duke was described in the *San Francisco Chronicle* as "politically imperishable" as sheriff.

The Sheriff's Office oversaw the jail, prisoner transportation to and from court hearings, the morgue, cattle branding, and weights and measures. Duke, and some of his brothers, were "naturals" for law enforcement careers—following in their late father's footsteps.

His campaign platform—delivered in both Hawaiian and English—was always the same: "We urgently need a new jail to replace the one we're in, built in 1857." He persevered, and a new one was built in 1962. The public trusted him, and while the Honolulu Police Department was rocked by wartime black market scandals, Duke ran a "tight ship."

Duke and Nadine were married at Mokuʻaikaua Church, Kailua-Kona.

*T*hat Boston teenager, Nadine Alexander, who had fallen in love with the handsome Duke's picture 20 years before? She had married and taught dancing in Europe.

In 1938, she was 33 years old, divorced, and working in New York City. When she was offered a dancing instructor position at the Royal Hawaiian Hotel, she said, "I didn't hesitate."

She settled in and soon had met all but two of the brothers. She told Sam she wanted to meet Duke, and he told her that Duke swam every day after work.

Nadine remembered, "My heart went pitty-pat when I saw him. . . . For me, it was love at first sight. He seemed more cautious, a confirmed bachelor. It took a few days for Duke to get up the courage to invite me to dinner. He was afraid I'd reject him, he told me later."

Duke's version: "One day, I was on the beach at Waikīkī and I saw her . . . it sort of struck me. Like, she's my girl. So I asked my brother Sam . . . to introduce me, and that was the beginning of our romance."

MRS. DUKE P. KAHANAMOKU
SECRETARY

During World War II, Nadine worked as a secretary and a mail censor.

*N*adine reminisced about their 27 years together:

"We dated for a few months. . . . Duke proposed by telephone. . . . Eight months later we married, on August 2, 1940. Our best man was Francis Hyde Iʻi Brown, and we honeymooned at his Kohala Coast estate.

"The accommodations made us laugh. There was a generator to make electricity. . . . We stayed in a sort of shed where Francis kept his fishing nets. It had a chest of drawers and two cots. Duke was over 6 feet tall and his feet hung over the end of the bed. We put the two cots together so we could be together. That didn't work, and we'd fall down in the middle.

"Every morning before the sun came up, Francis would throw stones on the roof to wake Duke. He'd jump up, have a cup of coffee, and the two of them would go out fishing. All day, every day. You'd think they were the honeymooners!

"Our friend Doris Duke helped us [buy a house] with an interest-free loan, as we had no money. We paid her back by monthly payments. Duke lived here the rest of his life."

The back entrance to Duke and Nadine's house at 114 Royal Circle, Honolulu.

While Europe was embroiled in war during 1939 and 1940, Nadine noted in her diary the creeping uneasiness Hawai'i felt. She jotted down how she and Duke watched tugs pulling firing practice targets off Waikīkī. They built a bomb shelter below their Black Point home, there were blackouts, and Nadine took advanced Red Cross training.

On Sunday December 7, 1941, at 7:55 A.M., Duke and Nadine were at the old Outrigger Canoe Club, their usual Sunday routine, before going fishing on their boat out of Pearl Harbor. Their breakfast was interrupted by an urgent phone call for the sheriff. He returned to the table to tell her, "Baby, we have to go. This is it."

When Hawai'i was attacked, martial law was declared. All able-bodied people were needed to help with the war effort. Nadine worked as a secretary for St. Andrew's Cathedral and also as a mail censor. Their beloved Great Dane grew so agitated from the constant sirens that he was put to sleep.

The Hawai'i Tourist Bureau closed, and hotels were commandeered by the military.

Duke's Boys, *left to right:* Thad Ekstrand, Jim Fernie, Carlos Rivas, Tommy Arnott, Tom O'Brien. Not pictured: John Beaumont, Bob Bush, Jim Pflueger.

*P*erhaps because he and Nadine had no children, Duke formed "Duke's Boys," an OCC paddling team, during the war. Duke was their steersman, and later, coach. The Boys were never defeated in nearly a decade of racing. Their senior-six canoe would be washed and stowed away before the second-place canoe came in.

Duke was their father figure. Under his guidance, the teenagers raked the OCC volleyball area, hauled sand, and planted *hau* tree cuttings. He instructed them to stay away from "beach trouble," sex, gambling, and fighting. There was no swearing or drinking when he was around.

They called him "Sir," "Pa," "Dad," and once in a while, "Duke." He called each of them "Kid."

Thad Ekstrand said, "We practiced every day after work, paddling the huge koa *Leilani* to Honolulu Harbor and back. Duke would holler, 'Stop, swim,' and we'd leap out in the middle of nowhere. Suddenly there was Duke taking off, pushing the stern, propelling it forward with his powerful kick. You'd have to swim hard to catch up with him.

Duke Wayne and Duke Kahanamoku in the 1948 sea epic *Wake of the Red Witch*. Wayne played a greedy sea captain and Duke played a native chief.

*I*n 1955 Duke was hospitalized with heart trouble. Hundreds of people worldwide put pen to paper to wish him a speedy recovery and to say, as did one admirer,

> You don't remember me, but I have never forgotten your kindness when you came up and spent 30 minutes with me [and showed me what I was doing wrong with my surfboard]. Only later I found out who you were when someone called your name. I never got to thank you. I was a homesick young soldier, stationed at Schofield Barracks 35 years ago.

In September, after his recovery, a Missouri newspaper headline read, "The Duke is Back on the Beach and All Is Well at Waikiki." The reporter wrote, "He still looked godlike a few days after his sixty-sixth birthday."

By November 1956, Duke had fully recovered and was delighted to attend the Melbourne Olympics as an official guest, and afterwards, to visit Freshie again and to ride his old board. Australia dropped his last name, and now simply called him "Dook."

Heiress Doris Duke with the six Kahanamoku brothers (Duke at far right), around 1937. She was an accomplished sailor, surfer, and swimmer.

*D*uke's lifelong friend Wilmer C. Morris recalls:

It was either Duke's 60th or 65th birthday, and we were sitting outside on the grass at his Black Point home on some mats.

All his brothers had arrived, and then Doris Duke joined us. Doris, "the richest girl in the world," for a long time was Sam Kahanamoku's girlfriend. During the course of the evening I had the opportunity to sit next to her, and talk to her, and you could tell by her expression and the way she looked at Duke that she really admired him, liked him.

So I said, "You really like Duke don't you?"

She said, "Yes, I do, you know, he has it all. He's known all over the world, and people admire him, and respect him, and with all that, he lives a very simple, uncomplicated life. He doesn't want a lot, certainly he's never asked me for anything."

CREED OF ALOHA

In Hawaii we greet friends, loved ones or strangers
With Aloha, which means with love.
Aloha is the key word to the universal spirit of real
hospitality, which makes Hawai'i renowned as the
world's center of understanding and fellowship.

Try meeting or leaving people with Aloha.
You'll be surprised by their reaction.
I believe it and it is my creed.
Aloha to you.

When Hawai'i became the fiftieth state in 1959, Duke's sheriff's position was abolished. He now became the official State of Hawai'i Ambassador of Aloha, which had been his lifelong crusade. He welcomed politicians at the wharf or airport, took celebrities canoeing or on around-O'ahu tours, was honorary marshal or honorary judge at countless events. He visited the Far East with Nadine. In Stockholm, he received the symbolic key to the city, where thousands remembered him from half a century before.

Duke Woefully Underpaid: Godfrey

By TOMI KNAEFLER

Entertainer Arthur Godfrey is "really burned up" at Hawaii for "the shabby treatment that Duke Kahanamoku is getting."

Godfrey, here to pick out television film sites, said in an interview:

"Hawaii should give Duke $25,000 a year and a car and require him to do nothing but appear at only the proper places."

When informed that Duke is on the City-County payroll ($8,256 a year as the City's official greeter), Godfrey said:

"Well, what he's getting is certainly not enough.

"It's a shame that he has to be the front man for a common restaurant just so he can get enough money to eat."

AT MARKET PLACE

Godfrey was referring to a restaurant which opens next month and will be called "Duke Kahanamoku's."

It will be located in a former section of Don the Beachcomber's at the In-

Turn to Page 2, Column 1

Godfrey, left, pictured as he was greeted on his recent arrival by Duke Kahanamoku.—United Air Lines Photo.

★ ★ ★

'I Think So Too,' Duke Says

By HELEN ALTONN

Duke Kahanamoku says he agrees with Arthur Godfrey that Hawaii is not treating him right "after I spent all my life selling Hawaii without pay."

The City's official greeter said it is true that "I am barely getting along.

"I agree that something should be done, but it is not my part to say anything.

"It takes a malihini (newcomer) like Arthur Godfrey to come here, look things over and speak the truth," he said.

SURPRISINGLY SMALL

Pulling out a paycheck, he noted, "I'm not getting the salary a lot of people think I'm getting. They

Turn to Page 2, Column 1

Honolulu Star-Bulletin, August 6, 1961.

*A*lways, Duke lived with aloha and promoted Hawai'i.

He was helped by his good friend Arthur Godfrey, whom he met in the 1940s when Godfrey was stationed with the navy in Hawai'i. Godfrey later became the most well known radio AND television personality in the United States. Through the 1950s and 1960s, Godfrey had helped publicize Hawai'i. He also helped Duke improve his financial condition by introducing him to manufacturers. Duke developed a line of aloha clothing, highly sought after by collectors today. The *New York Post* called its bright hues "Hawai'i Hallucinations." Everyone—crooner Bing Crosby, President Harry Truman—started wearing them. They were casual and could be worn over a belt. The straight cut along the bottom seam was Duke's idea.

By 2004, surf clothing would be a $6 billion industry forever linked to Hawaiian designs.

They had a pact: whoever died first, the other would deliver his friend's eulogy.

Duke outside his restaurant, wearing one of his brightly hued Duke Kahanamoku aloha shirts.

*D*uke joined with some entrepreneurs to launch Duke Kahanamoku's, at the International Market Place on Kalākaua Avenue, in the early 1960s. It became one of the most popular tourist luaus and watering holes. Duke was the official greeter. The restaurant added little to his financial security.

Adulation greeted Duke wherever he went. Here he arrives at LAX in 1966 for the International Surfing Hall of Fame Awards. He was the first inductee.

*D*uke's fame never diminished like many sports heroes'. A sportswriter wrote how he watched a surfer stare at Duke, then go up to him, reach out and tentatively touch his arm. When Duke turned around, the lad apologized, and said, "I just wanted to touch you."

Even legends like Joe Quigg and Ben R. Finney have said that they felt Duke's *mana* and feared approaching him. When Duke, George "Dad" Center, and John D. Kaupiko appeared on the beach, "everything went quiet," rascals stopped misbehaving, said John M. Lind. They controlled Waikīkī. There was a pecking order, like chiefs of old. If they hollered, "Hey kid, go in the baby surf," everyone did what they said.

•••

"We hosted the West Coast Surfing Championships at Huntington Beach [California] in 1962. There must have been 10,000 kids on the beach, all kinds of little gremmies, and when Duke stepped out of the car it was like God had arrived. I couldn't believe the adulation," said Kimo Wilder McVay.

Seventy-one-year-old Duke shows his fighting spirit during recuperation from critical brain surgery in 1962.

*I*n 1962, Duke underwent brain surgery to remove a debilitating clot, but made a remarkable recovery. From then until the day he died, Duke stayed busy.

He said, "I like the feel of the fresh air and the salt water. I believe in keeping active."

He had graduated from a surfboard to various kinds of sailing craft, including a catamaran, and finally a powerboat built to his specifications, called the *Nadu K,* a combination of his and Nadine's names with a pleasant Hawaiian sound to it.

One of Duke's last formal photographs, to raise money for Easter Seals Hawai'i.

*D*uke had no interest in a statue and authorized only a posthumously published biography. He was pleased, though, to see a foundation established during his lifetime to help scholar-athletes.

Surfer interviewed the Father of International Surfing in 1965 and asked him,

Q: Do you have any tips you'd like to pass along to young surfers?

A: Duke: "I think we have to teach a lot of these kids to first be gentlemen. . . . Try to help one another and not hog the doggone waves.

"You know, there are so many waves coming in all the time, you don't have to worry about that. Just take your time—wave comes. Let the other guys go; catch another one.

"And that's what we used to do. We'd see some other fella there first, and we'd say, 'You're here first. You take the first wave.' "

To Duke, waiting for a wave was simply another example of Hawaiian *waipahē*, courtesy, gentlemanliness.

Nadine reminisces in 1996, at Duke's Canoe Club, about the time she and Duke taught the Queen Mother to dance hula (see framed photo just above Nadine's head).

*D*uke's 76th birthday cake featured a picture of him dancing an impromptu hula with Queen Elizabeth, the Queen Mother. It came about this way:

She was en route from Australia to London and landed for airplane refueling. Greeted with Hawaiian music, the Queen Mum surprised everyone. She told Gov. John A. Burns that she felt like dancing. Burns summoned Duke and Nadine, and the 65-year-old Queen Mum imitated their movements. The photograph appeared in newspapers worldwide.

For his birthday Duke also received a plaque from the Hawaii Visitors Bureau. "We give you this plaque," said Bob Allen, "because you made the HVB possible." An out-of-town reporter described him as "the only living legend in the world."

The next year, just three weeks before his death, Duke welcomed the millionth visitor to Hawai'i. Tourism was now Hawai'i's major industry, bringing in about $375 million every year.

Duke at 77, about three weeks before his death.

*D*uke collapsed at Waikiki Yacht Club on January 22, 1968, not far from Kālia, and died soon after.

He was the greatest aquatic sportsman the world has ever seen—father of U.S. modern swimming and international surfing, a champion diver, bodysurfer, water polo player, surfboard polo player, fisherman, paddler, yachtsman, and sailor.

At least 45 water-related events or places are named for him.

"The only question for history is how big Duke's legend will become" we [the *Honolulu Advertiser*] said . . . two years ago. Some of the things bearing his name include a scholarship foundation, a beach, a swimming pool at the university, an annual regatta, a restaurant and a nightspot, a line of sportswear, a music and recording company, ukuleles, surfboards, a surfing club, and an international surfing championship.

But far more important is perpetuating Duke's spirit—the friendly, modest young Hawaiian boy whose real accomplishments won the respect of the world, the older man who carried his legend with modest dignity. These are goals all might seek.

Duke must always be a part of Hawai'i. . . . We must never lose him in spirit later.

'It'll Never Be the Same.'

*D*IED: Duke Kahanamoku, 77, Hawaiʻi's fabled swimmer, surfer and all-round citizen . . . his name might as well have been King. . . . Age never daunted him. To the last, he was a symbol of the islands, surfing, swimming, and appearing as the 50th state's official greeter.

Time magazine

Spark Matsunaga told Congress:

Just as Diamond Head symbolized the geography of Hawaiʻi, Duke symbolized the people of Hawaiʻi.

More than any other individual, he represented what other people throughout the world picture the true Hawaiian to be—friendly, cheerful, athletic, tall, and handsome—someone you wanted to get to know better. He made you proud to even be just an acquaintance of his.

The legendary Duke sold Hawaiʻi to the world and in so doing became a citizen of the world. Hawaiʻi, the United States and the whole human race have lost a true champion and a rare specimen of a man.

'Don't Wipe Out, Bruddah'

An editorial cartoon published on the day of Duke's funeral, reminding readers how much Duke meant to Hawai'i and the world.

*A*rthur Godfrey delivered the eulogy at Duke's funeral five days later.

> Duke was the soul of dignity . . . but he could be a mischievous, delightful boy at heart. . . . He was unassuming, reticent, almost shy . . . . Flattery rolled off his back like spume from a wave . . . . He retreated from fawning phonies, politely but firmly. . . . It was the wonderful world of water that gave Duke his relaxed, enviable peace of mind. . . . That great physical strength alone would never have won those titles for him. . . . He had known defeat but he had persevered with great courage.

Beach boy ceremonies were held on the beach in front of the Royal Hawaiian Hotel, near where Duke had surfed, trained, swum, frolicked, played ukulele, first met Nadine.

Waikīkī was so muted, and dark, it was almost unrecognizable. Storm clouds hovered while the outrigger canoes paddled out beyond the reef. Rain, tears, and spray comingled and streamed down mourners' faces.

The canoes formed an embracing circle, as Duke's ashes and lei tributes were placed in the sea.

Duke returned home.

$\mathcal{N}$otes

page 3   The beautiful phrase "Vikings of the Sunrise" was coined
              by Sir Peter Buck (Te Rangi Hiroa).

page 5   The figure "800,000 to 1 million in 1778" is from David
              E. Stannard, *Before the Horror* (Honolulu: Social Science
              Research Institute, University of Hawai'i, 1989). The fig-
              ure "82,000 in 1850" is from Andrew W. Lind, *Hawaii's
              People* (Honolulu: University of Hawai'i Press, 1967), p. 8.

page 7   The definitions of *aloha* are from Mary Kawena Pukui and
              Samuel H. Elbert, *Hawaiian Dictionary*, rev. and enl. ed.
              (Honolulu: University of Hawai'i Press, 1986), p. 21.

page 9   HRH Duke of Edinburgh's visit was described in *Pacific
              Commercial Advertiser*, July 24, 1869.

page 11   Fittingly, since Duke was Hawai'i's first Olympian, this
              chant welcomed triathletes to Hawai'i's first-ever Olympic
              pre-trials, April 16, 2004.

page 21   Duke's comments about learning to swim are from
              Thomas G. Thrum, *All About Hawai'i,* compiled and edit-
              ed by Charles E. Frankel, 89th ed. (Honolulu: Star-
              Bulletin Printing Co., 1967), p. 169.

page 25   The proverb *"Ku no i ke ke'a"* is from Mary Kawena
              Pukui, coll., ed., ann., *'Ōlelo No'eau: Hawaiian Proverbs
              and Poetical Sayings*, Bernice P. Bishop Museum Special
              Publication No. 71 (Honolulu: Bishop Museum Press,
              1983), p. 206.

page 27   Duke's siblings were David Piikoi, Bernice Pauahi
              Kahaleula, William Puuku, Samuel Alapai, Julia
              Kapiolani, Maria Halapu, Louis Kooliko, and Sargent
              Hiikua.

page 31   From AAU President Otto Wahle's letter, quoted in the
              Pacific Commercial Advertiser, Nov. 10, 1911.

page 33	*Los Angeles Times*, July 16, 1916.
page 35	Grant Rodwell and John Ramsland, "Cecil Healy: A Soldier of the Surf," *Sporting Traditions* (16/2, May 2000). Healy died in World War I.
page 37	*Honolulu Star-Bulletin,* Oct. 1, 1912.
page 39	*Pacific Commercial Advertiser*, June 9, 1913.
page 47	*Los Angeles Times,* Jan. 18, 1917; *Honolulu Star-Bulletin*, Sept. 6 and 7, 1917; note handwritten by Duke in 1963, Hawai'i State Archives.
page 49	*Pacific Commercial Advertiser*, March 17, 1918, p. 1. The all-Hawaiian trio were Duke, Clarence Lane, and Stubby Kruger.
page 53	Author interview, Nov. 2002. Viola, who was diving well into her 90s, died at age 102 as this book went to press. Her first husband was Fred Cady, an Olympic diving coach and a close friend of Duke's. After Cady's death, Viola married Fred Krahn.
page 57	*The New York Times*, July 22, 1924, p. 10.
page 59	The account of the rescue is from the *Honolulu Star-Bulletin* April 18, 1953. Duke Kahanamoku, with Joe Brennan, *World of Surfing* (New York: Grosset and Dunlap, 1968).
page 61	The account of Duke's christening of the Natatorium is from the *Honolulu Advertiser*, Aug. 27, 1927. The account of Duke's City Hall job is from the *Honolulu Star-Bulletin*, Feb. 18, 1933.
page 63	Gary Lynch and Malcolm Gault-Williams, *Tom Blake in Hawaii, 1924–1955* (Corona del Mar, CA: Croul Family Foundation, 2002), p. 1.
page 65	Lynch and Gault-Williams, page ix. Will Connolly, *San Francisco Chronicle*, Dec. 3, 1958.
page 67	Will Connolly, *San Francisco Chronicle*, Dec. 3, 1958.
page 68	Will Connolly, *San Francisco Chronicle*, Dec. 3, 1958.

page 71	Bob Krauss, *Honolulu Advertiser*, Aug. 3, 1965. Author interview with Nadine Kahanamoku, 1993.
page 73	Author interview with Nadine Kahanamoku, 1993. Nadine died at age 92, in 1997. She left their now sizable estate to the University of Hawai'i John A. Burns School of Medicine to help Hawaiian medical students. Those who receive scholarshiops are known as Kahanamoku Scholars.
page 75	Author interview with Nadine Kahanamoku, 1993.
page 77	Author interviews with Thad Ekstrand, Sept./Oct. 2003.
page 79	Letter in Hawai'i State Archives. Bob Considine, *St. Louis Post-Dispatch*, Sept. 10, 1956.
page 83	Letter to author from Wilmer C. Morris, Sept. 2003.
page 85	The Surf Industry Manufacturers Association provided 2004 estimates of $4.4 million U.S. and $6 billion world-wide.
page 89	Anecdote about the admiring surfer is from Hal Wood, *Honolulu Star-Bulletin and Advertiser*, March 12, 1967, B6. Author interviews with University of Hawai'i Dept. of Anthropology Prof. Emeritus Ben R. Finney; board shaper Joe Quigg; John M. Lind, Waikīkī Surf Club/Makaha International Surf Contest. Greg Ambrose interview with Kimo Wilder McVay, 1995.
page 93	*Surfer* Magazine, March 1965.
page 95	*Honolulu Star-Bulletin*, Jan. 23, 1968, A33. *Houston Chronicle,* April 1966.
page 97	*Honolulu Advertiser* Jan. 23, 1968, B2.
page 99	*TIME* Magazine, Feb. 2, 1968. Then U.S. Representative, later U.S. Senator Spark Matsunaga, U.S. Congressional Record—House, 90th Congress, 2nd Session, Jan. 23, 1968.
page 101	Arthur Godfrey, "Memories of a Great Man," *Beacon*, Aug. 1968.

$\mathcal{P}$hoto Credits

page 48	*Pacific Commercial Advertiser,* March 17, 1918, p. 1/ Hawai'i DLNR/SHPD.
page 50	The Academy of Motion Picture Arts and Sciences.
page 52	Paragon Agency.
page 54	Hawai'i State Archives.
page 56	Photographer unknown. International Swimming Hall of Fame.
page 58	The Academy of Motion Picture Arts and Sciences.
page 60	*Honolulu Star-Bulletin,* July 26, 1934, p. 5/Hawai'i DLNR/SHPD.
page 62	Croul Family Foundation.
page 64	© Clarence Maki.
page 66	Hawai'i State Archives.
page 68	Nadine A. Kahanamoku/Sandra Kimberley Hall.
page 70	Burl Burlingame Airchive.
page 72	Nadine A. Kahanamoku/Sandra Kimberley Hall.
page 74	Sandra Kimberley Hall, 1997.
page 76	Thad Ekstrand.
page 78	The Academy of Motion Picture Arts and Sciences.
page 80	Jo-Anne Kahanamoku, Sam Kahanamoku's daughter.
page 82	*Pacific Commercial Advertiser*/Hawai'i DLNR/SHPD.
page 84	*Honolulu Star-Bulletin,* Aug. 6, 1961, p. 1. *Honolulu Star-Bulletin*/Hawai'i DLNR/SHPD.
page 86	Sandra Kimberley Hall Archive.
page 88	Press photographer unknown.
page 90	Sandra Kimberley Hall Archive.
page 92	Easter Seals Hawai'i.
page 94	Sandra Kimberley Hall Archive.
page 96	LeRoy "Granny" Grannis.
page 98	*Honolulu Advertiser*/Hawai'i DLNR/SHPD.
page 100	*Honolulu Advertiser,* Jan. 27, 1968.
page 102	Earl Maikahikinapāmaikalā Tenn.

For Further Reading

Blake, Tom. *Hawaiian Surfriders, 1935*. Redondo Beach, CA: Mountain and Sea Publishing, 1983.

Brennan, Joe. *Duke of Hawai'i*. New York: Ballantine Books, 1968.

Buck, Peter (Te Rangi Hiroa). *Vikings of the Sunrise*. New York: F. A. Stokes, 1938.

Cole, Margery Voyer. *Viola: Diving Wonder and Aquatic Champion*. Orange, CA: Paragon Agency, 2001.

DelaVega, Timothy, et al. *200 Years of Surfing Literature: A Bibliography*. Hanapepe, Hawai'i: DelaVega, 2004.

Hall, Sandra Kimberley, and Greg Ambrose. *Memories of Duke: The Legend Comes to Life*. Honolulu: Bess Press, 1995.

Hope, Dale. With Gregory Tozian. *The Aloha Shirt*. Hillsboro, OR: Beyond Words Publishing, 2000.

Kahanamoku, Duke, with Joe Brennan. *Duke Kahanamoku's World of Surfing*. New York: Grosset & Dunlap, 1968.

Kanahele, George Hu'eu Sanford. Ku Kanaka *Stand Tall: A Search for Hawaiian Values*. Honolulu: University of Hawai'i Press, 1986.

Lynch, Gary, and Malcolm Gault-Williams. *Tom Blake in Hawai'i, 1924–1955*. Corona del Mar, CA: Croul Family Foundation. 2002.

Margan, Frank, and Ben R. Finney. *A Pictorial History of Surfing*. Dee Why West, NSW: Hamlyn, 1970.

Noyes, Martha H. *Then There Were None*. Honolulu: Bess Press. 2003.

Warshaw, Matt. *Encyclopedia of Surfing*. Orlando, Florida: Harcourt, Inc., 2003.

$\mathcal{I}$ndex

Each day, thousands visit Duke's Waikīkī statue, designed by Jan Fisher, and ponder his Creed of Aloha at its base.